GET INTO

GET-INTO-IT
GUIDES

DIORAMAS
AND MODELS

JANICE DYER

CRABTREE
Publishing Company
www.crabtreebooks.com

Author: Janice Dyer

Editors:
Marcia Abramson, Philip Gebhardt, Janine Deschenes

Photo research: Melissa McClellan

Editorial director: Kathy Middleton

Proofreader: Wendy Scavuzzo

Cover/Interior Design: T.J. Choleva

**Production coordinator and
  Prepress technician:** Samara Parent

Print coordinator: Katherine Berti

Consultant: Sarah Hodgson – Art and New Media
teacher, Hamilton-Wentworth District School Board

Developed and produced for Crabtree Publishing
by BlueApple*Works* Inc.

Project Designers
Diorama on page 22 – Joshua Avramson; diorama on page 24 – Melissa
McClellan; models on pages 26, 28 – Janet Compare-Fritz

Photographs

Shutterstock.com: © Marianoblanco (title page); © Happy Together (TOC);
© CandyBox Images (p. 4 middle); © TAGSTOCK1 (p. 5 left); © RoyStudioEU
(p. 5 background); © Nikonaft (p. 5 bottom right); © windu (p. 6 top left);
© koya979 (p. 6 top 2cd from left); © Elena Elisseeva (p. 6 top middle);
© Everything (p. 6 top right); © Paul Turner (p. 6 bottom left); © kaspan (p. 6
bottom right); © Shchipkova Elena (p. 8 top right); © AustralianCamera (p. 8
bottom right); © PR Image Factory (p. 10 top right); © Nattika (p. 11 bottom);
© Fotana (p. 11 right); © rzstudio (p. 13 top right); © donatas1205 (p. 16 top
left); © Sergei Kardashev (p. 16 bottom left inset); © saknakorn (p. 16 bottom
right inset); © Galushko Sergey (p. 18 bottom right); © Pavel Vakhrushev (p. 19
bottom left); © pun photo (p. 19 bottom right); © Salparadis (p. 22--23 top); ©
Billion Photos (p. 24–25 top); © Monkey Business Images (p. 25 bottom right),
© Cuson (p. 26–27 top); © Stavrida (p. 28–29); © SergiyN (p. 29 bottom left); ©
Early Spring (p. 29 bottom right);

Keystone Press: © Eric Engman/News-Miner (p. 5 top right);

© Austen Photogrpahy (cover insets, p. 6 bottom middle, 9, 10, 12, 13, 14, 15, 18,
19, 20, 21, 22, 23, 24, 25, 26, 27, back cover);

© Sam Taylor (cover children, p. 4 left, 4 right, 8 left, 11 bottom, 15 bottom right,
19 top middle, 21 bottom left);

Public Domain: Lewis Carroll (p. 24, 25, 32)

Library and Archives Canada Cataloguing in Publication

Dyer, Janice, author
    Get into dioramas and models / Janice Dyer.

(Get-into-it guides)
Includes index.
Issued in print and electronic formats.
ISBN 978-0-7787-2640-1 (hardback).--ISBN 978-0-7787-2646-3
(paperback).--ISBN 978-1-4271-1791-5 (html)

    1. Models and modelmaking--Juvenile literature. I. Title.

TT154 D94 2016   j745.5928   C2016-903389-9
                                           C2016-903390-2

Library of Congress Cataloging-in-Publication Data

Names: Dyer, Janice, author.
Title: Get into dioramas and models / Janice Dyer.
Description: St. Catharines, Ontario ; New York, New York : Crabtree
  Publishing Company, [2016] | Series: Get-into-it guides | Audience: Ages
  8-11. | Audience: Grades 4 to 6.
Identifiers: LCCN 2016026909 (print) | LCCN 2016028752 (ebook) | ISBN
  9780778726401 (reinforced library binding : alk. paper) | ISBN
  9780778726463 (pbk. : alk. paper) | ISBN 9781427117915 (Electronic HTML)
Subjects: LCSH: Diorama--Juvenile literature. | Models and
  modelmaking--Juvenile literature. | Handicraft--Juvenile literature.
Classification: LCC ND2880 .D94 2016 (print) | LCC ND2880 (ebook) | DDC
  745.8--dc23
LC record available at https://lccn.loc.gov/2016026909

Crabtree Publishing Company

www.crabtreebooks.com   1-800-387-7650

Printed in Canada/072016/EF20160630

Published in Canada
Crabtree Publishing
616 Welland Ave.
St. Catharines, Ontario
L2M 5V6

Published in the United States
Crabtree Publishing
PMB 59051
350 Fifth Avenue, 59th Floor
New York, New York 10118

Published in the United Kingdom
Crabtree Publishing
Maritime House
Basin Road North, Hove
BN41 1WR

Published in Australia
Crabtree Publishing
3 Charles Street
Coburg North
VIC, 3058

CONTENTS

WHAT ARE DIORAMAS AND MODELS?

Dioramas are **three-dimensional** (3-D) scenes. The scenes fit inside a frame, and are made with many different kinds of materials. They are used to tell a story, or capture a moment in time. Model train enthusiasts use dioramas to create **authentic** countryside scenery to make their train layout look realistic. Students often use dioramas to show historical events, or for science fair projects.

Models are **representations** of real things. You can build and use a 3-D model to show something on its own, or you can add models to a diorama to create a scene. For example, adding models of airplanes to a diorama of an airport will help you create a realistic scene.

Teachers and students often use dioramas and models. They make great science fair projects.

Miniatures or Enlargements

Some dioramas are much bigger or smaller than real life. If you create a diorama to show a historical event, it will be a miniature representation of the scene. Scientists use enlarged models to study human cells in detail. Museums use life-sized dioramas to show scenes, animals, and people in different places, times, and **habitats**.

How to Use this Book

The projects in this book are meant to inspire you to create your own models and dioramas. You can follow the steps provided, or use your imagination to add your own new ideas to the project.

Did You Know?

The Washington Post *has held a diorama contest since 2007. Every year, more than 700 people submit a diorama made of marshmallow PEEPS® candy. They also use fabric, paint, cardboard, and other materials to create their incredible scenes.*

How are Models Used?

Artists use painting and carvings to create miniature scenes. Scientists use models to learn about things that are too big, too small, or too **complex** to study in real life. Doctors show patients 3-D models of parts of the body so patients understand their condition. Architects also use models to show how their designs will look once they are built.

SOURCES AND MATERIALS

You probably have many of the basic supplies for building models and dioramas, such as cardboard, paint, crayons, scraps of fabric, clay, buttons, beads, glue, string, and scissors. At a craft store or dollar store, you can purchase other materials, such as plastic animals and figures, moss, and other types of greenery.

RECYCLABLES

You can make many of the models and dioramas in this book with materials found around the house. Instead of throwing out or recycling objects, save them to use in your projects. You can use newspapers, egg cartons, cardboard boxes, mailing tubes, cereal and tissue boxes, tin cans, empty toilet paper and paper towel rolls, and more. Just use your imagination!

Empty paper towel rolls

Store-bought or hand-picked nature elements

Recycled containers

Boxes with or without lids

Old newspapers and magazines

MATERIALS NEEDED

Most dioramas start with a box, which becomes the base and background for your project. Clean pizza boxes are great for creating dioramas with backgrounds, or you can turn a shoe box on its side. After you have your base, use your imagination to create a colorful diorama!

If you follow the steps for the projects, you will need these materials.

RAINFOREST DIORAMA
PAGE 22

- ✔ box
- ✔ twigs
- ✔ glue
- ✔ moss
- ✔ tissue paper
- ✔ figurines (clay or plastic)
- ✔ paint
- ✔ vines
- ✔ stones
- ✔ colored sand
- ✔ flowers and other greenery

ALICE IN WONDERLAND DIORAMA
PAGE 24

- ✔ box
- ✔ paper
- ✔ card stock
- ✔ colored pencils or markers
- ✔ scissors
- ✔ glue or double-sided tape
- ✔ paint
- ✔ old magazines or photos of background images and characters
- ✔ old playing cards

YOUR FAVORITE DOG PARK MODEL
PAGE 26

- ✔ materials for paper mache (see page 12)
- ✔ cardboard
- ✔ pebbles
- ✔ paint
- ✔ stir sticks
- ✔ glue
- ✔ plastic netting from food containers or produce bags
- ✔ plastic wrap
- ✔ tissue paper
- ✔ plastic or clay dogs

YOUR DREAM HOUSE MODEL
PAGE 28

- ✔ materials for paper mache (see page 12)
- ✔ card stock
- ✔ waxed paper or plastic wrap
- ✔ tissue paper
- ✔ paint
- ✔ colored salt
- ✔ cardboard
- ✔ glue
- ✔ pasta
- ✔ twigs and moss
- ✔ wild rice

To make colored salt:

Fill a recycled plastic container with salt, add food coloring, and stir until all the salt is dyed. Keep adding the food coloring until you have the desired color.

DESIGNING AND PLANNING YOUR SCENE

How do you decide what kind of model or diorama to make? Start by thinking of a topic or idea that interests you. Do you want to show a scene in a book? A period in time? An **ecosystem** or animal habitat?

You can also look for an image or scene that you like in a book or magazine, or on a website. You can recreate the scene as is, or use your imagination to add to it or change it. The possibilities are endless!

Once you have an idea for your project, follow these steps to plan your scene.

Animal habitats are popular subjects for dioramas.

GATHER YOUR MATERIALS

Make a list of all the things you want to include in your diorama. Collect the materials that you will need ahead of time. This will make it easier to build your project. Consider:

○ Do you have everything you need, or do you need to purchase any supplies?

○ What techniques will you use? Painting? Cutting and pasting? Creating objects with clay? Make sure you have all the materials you will need.

Scaling it Right

Next, think about the scale you will use. A scale is a comparison between the size of an object in real life and the size of the model of the object. For example, if you are building a diorama of a train yard, the model train will be much smaller than a real train. If your train's locomotive is 2 inches (5 cm) long, you will need to make the train station much bigger than the locomotive, as it is in real life.

Sketch the Scene

Once you decide on the scale, make a rough sketch of the scene. Think about where you will place each element of the diorama. You might want to place taller figures in the back, and medium and shorter items in the front.

You don't want the people in your diorama to be bigger than the house!

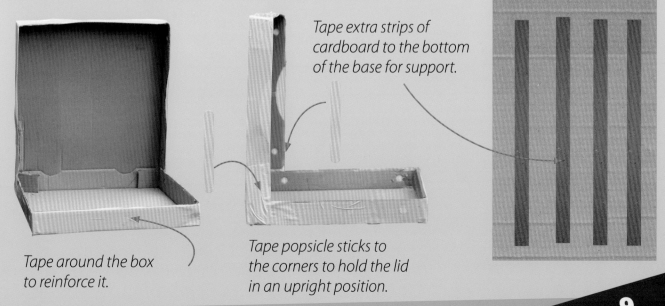

BUILD A SUPPORT FOR YOUR BOXES

Sometimes you might need to make the box or model base stronger. If you are using a pizza box, tape popsicle sticks to each side to hold the lid upright. You may also need to tape additional pieces of cardboard to the bottom of your model base to make the base sturdier.

Tape extra strips of cardboard to the bottom of the base for support.

Tape around the box to reinforce it.

Tape popsicle sticks to the corners to hold the lid in an upright position.

WORKING WITH PAPER

You can choose to use paper to create all the figures and scenery for your diorama. When cutting detailed shapes, cut with scissors carefully around the lines for the best result. Sometimes it is easier to first cut out the overall shape, then cut out the details.

FOLDING AND BENDING

Use tabs to glue figures or other features such as trees to the box. Cut the tabs out with the figure as one piece if you are using card stock. If your figure is cut out from thinner paper, glue the card stock tab to the figure, then the tab to the box.

Add a narrow strip of cardboard or card stock to the back of the figure to help it stand upright.

Thin-paper figure with card stock tab glued on

How Tabs Work

Glue or tape to figure.

Glue or tape to box.

You can use tabs to attach the figure to the bottom, the side, or even the top of the box.

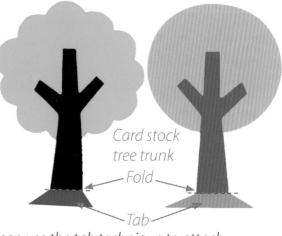

Card stock tree trunk

Fold

Tab

You can use the tab technique to attach paper trees to your project. Cut out tree shapes from paper and trunks from card stock. Glue the tree top to the tree trunk. Fold the bottom of the trunk to create a tab.

Create flowers by crumpling bits of tissue paper and gluing them to the base.

Create trees by crumpling tissue paper and wrapping it around a tree base made of paper mache, a drinking straw, or a twig.

Create water by cutting out blue tissue paper into the shape of the water feature. Glue it to the base, then cover with a thick layer of clear glue.

Using Collage

Once you have a basic structure for your diorama, you can use collage techniques to add features such as sky, grass, mountains, or water.

1 *Cut out images from old magazines, or use torn pieces of tissue paper.*

2 ***Dilute*** *craft glue with a little water. Make sure the label on the glue says it dries clear. Use a paintbrush to spread some glue onto a small part of your project. Press the paper into the glue. Repeat until you have covered the entire area.*

3 *When you are finished gluing the paper, cover it with a thin layer of glue to seal the paper.*

Using Markers, Colored Pencils, and Paint

Use markers, watercolor paint, or colored pencils to color cutouts of trees, structures, and figures for a paper diorama. Make sure to put newspaper or a flattened cardboard box under your work area. Draw or print out your objects and figures, then paint or color them before cutting them out.

Cross Hatching

Cross hatching is a technique for coloring large solid areas with pencils. Draw lines going in one direction. Then draw over them making lines that cross them in another direction.

PAPER MACHE

Paper mache is made of a mixture of strips of paper and glue, or paper, flour, and water. When it dries, it becomes hard. You can make all kinds of objects for your diorama with paper mache.

Paper mache is really easy to do. You don't need a lot of materials. Start by preparing your choice of glue, and making newspaper strips. Tear the newspaper pages into strips about 1 inch (2.5 cm) wide by 4 inches (10 cm) long. Make a big pile of strips. And now the fun begins!

PAPER MACHE TECHNIQUE

Before you start applying paper strips, prepare your mold and shapes for the bases. You can create forms from crumpled newspapers and cardboard products, bowls, plates, or balloons. Paper towel rolls and pipe cleaners work well, too. Balloons are great for round shapes because they will tear away from your dried paper mache easily when burst. When using bowls or plates, cover them with a thin layer of Vaseline first to stop the paper mache from sticking to them.

Once your molds are ready, it is time to apply the paper strips. Cover the strips of paper with glue on both sides with a paintbrush. Then place your strips one at a time over the mold, smoothing the strips to remove any air bubbles. Cover the mold with two or three layers at a time. If you put too many layers on at once, it will take too long to dry. Build up the layers until you have the thickness you want.

When completely dry, cover your creation with two coats of paint to seal it. You can use any type of paint, but the most popular paint is water-based acrylic. It is easy to use, and it dries quickly.

WHAT YOU WILL NEED

- ✔ large mixing bowl (8 cup or 2 l)
- ✔ newspaper
- ✔ 1 cup (250 ml) flour or glue
- ✔ 3 tablespoons (45 ml) salt
- ✔ 2 cups (500 ml) water
- ✔ measuring cup
- ✔ spoon

Paper Mache Glue - Made with Flour

Add flour and salt to a bowl and add water slowly, mixing with a spoon. Continue to add water until your paste is like a thin pancake batter—smooth with no lumps.

Paper Mache Glue - Made with Glue

Add 1 cup (250 ml) white glue and 2 cups (500 ml) water to a bowl. Mix together with a spoon until the mixture is well blended.

PAPER MACHE FEATURES FOR THE COMMUNITY SCENE, PAGE 26

HILL FEATURE

1 Blow up a small balloon to just a bit smaller size than you want your hill feature to be. Keep in mind you will only be using half of this balloon shape.

2 Cover your balloon with paper strips covered in glue. Smooth each layer out with your fingers. Helpful hint: Cover the balloon with strips in one direction, then add a second layer **perpendicular** to the first layer.

PAGE 26

Did You Know?

Throughout history, people have used paper mache for many different purposes. It was used to make small boxes, masks, trays, and other crafts, and to decorate armor and shields and architecture. In the 1800s, a type of paper mache was even used to build canoes!

3 Once your balloon is covered to the thickness you want, hang it to dry. This may take 24 hours.

4 Blow up four more balloons, each balloon smaller than the previous one. These will be used for your steps. Once you have all parts ready and dry, cut the shapes as shown above and glue them together.

5 Paint your hill to seal it and to hide the newspaper material.

OTHER FEATURES

Twig covered in paper mache to form a tree trunk

Pipe cleaners used as hoops

Cut cardboard tube used as a base for the tunnel element

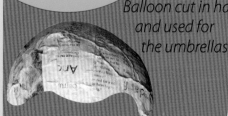

Balloon cut in half, shaped, and used for the umbrellas

Scrunched-up paper used as a mold for the climbing tower

MODELING CLAY CHARACTERS

Air-dry clay is a great material to use to create human and animal figures, and many other objects for your diorama. You can also use modeling clay to create your figures. With modeling clay, you don't have to wait for the clay to dry. Make sure you make the figures to scale so that they fit in your diorama or beside your model.

HOW TO MAKE A HUMAN FIGURE WITH AIR-DRY CLAY

1 *Start by kneading the clay in your hands to warm it up and soften it. Take a pinch of clay and roll it into a smooth ball for the head.*

2 *Take a bigger pinch of clay and form it into a rough rectangle for the body.*

3 *Take two small pinches of clay to make the arms, then two more for the legs. Attach them to the body.*

4 *Connect the head to the body. If it doesn't look right, fix it however you want.*

5 *Use other colors of clay to make the face, hair, clothes, or anything else you want to add. You can also paint the clay once it is dry.*

6 *Let the clay dry before placing the figure in your diorama.*

HOW TO MAKE A HUMAN FIGURE WITH MODELING CLAY

WHAT YOU WILL NEED

✔ air-dry clay or modeling clay
✔ cardboard or foam board
✔ rolling pin
✔ paint
✔ googly eyes

1. Use steps 1-4 as described above to form the base for the body.
2. Instead of painting the clay, use small pieces of modeling clay to form the detailed features such as hair, eyes, mouth, and clothes. Add store-bought googly eyes if you wish.
3. Add the decorative parts to the base as you see fit, and smooth the connection points with your fingers.

HOW TO MAKE AN ANIMAL FIGURE

1 Knead the clay in your hands to soften it and to warm it up.

2 To create an oval shape for the body, roll a large piece of clay in your hand, then roll it on a flat surface to smooth.

TIP
Working with Modeling Clay
Modeling clay is oily and can be messy to work with. Prepare a work area. A piece of cardboard or foam board is great to work on. Wash your hands well when you finish working, since they will be oily, too.

3 Make a ball for the head by moving your hands in a circle while pressing the clay lightly between them. Make a nose by pinching and rolling one end of the ball into a point.

8 Paint on eyes, a nose, a mouth, and a black tip on the tail, or use different colors of clay to make the details.

7 Attach the pieces together. Press the body into the legs. Press the head onto the body. Press the ears onto the head. Press the tail into the back end of the body.

4 Make four legs by separating a large piece of clay into four equal pieces. Roll each piece in your hands, then roll it on a flat surface to smooth it. Press each end onto the table to flatten it.

6 To make the tail, roll a small piece of clay on a flat surface with your fingers.

5 Make two ears by separating a small piece of clay into two equal pieces. Roll each piece into a ball and flatten it between your thumb and fingers. Press one end of each ear into a point.

MAKING OTHER ANIMALS

Use the same technique to make other animals. Look at a photo of the animal or bird to get the basic shape.

CREATING THE GROUND

Building up the ground or floor of your scene is an important part of creating a realistic diorama. Begin by adding your first layer of details and objects at the back and on the sides of your diorama. Grass or snow features, pebbled pathways or sand features, or mountains and hills, will make the scene more lifelike. Here's how!

TECHNIQUES FOR CREATING GRASS FEATURES

Paint the base.

Cover the base with fabric, felt, or green tissue paper.

Mix green paint with coarse salt to make textured paint. Paint a layer of glue on the base and then cover with the textured paint.

TECHNIQUES FOR CREATING SNOW FEATURES

Use Styrofoam to create icebergs or a snowy landscape.

Use cotton balls to create snow effects.

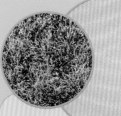

TIP

An easy way to create grass is to cut a picture from a photo or magazine and glue it to the bottom of your diorama. You can also make a collage of different pictures of grass. You can use the same technique to create sand features or pathways.

16

TECHNIQUES FOR CREATING SAND FEATURES AND PEBBLED PATHWAYS

Use small stones or pebbles to create pebbled pathways.

Glue sandpaper, real sand, or bird seed to the bottom of the frame.

Glue multi-colored wild rice to the base to create great-looking walkways or driveways.

TECHNIQUES FOR CREATING BACKGROUNDS

Cut out and glue paper shapes to create hill shapes.

Paint a mountain or hill as the background of the scene.

Glue a photo of a mountain or hill to the background.

ADDING SHRUBS AND GREENERY

Shrubs, greenery, and flowers add detail and help make your diorama more realistic. You can purchase plastic shrubs, flowers, and grasses from a dollar store, or you can find real ones in a garden. Place the objects where you want them, in groups or on their own.

There are several ways to add shrubs to your diorama or model. You can stick them in clay so they don't fall over, stick them in moss if it's thick enough, or glue them to the bottom if they have their own base.

CREATING NATURE FEATURES

Moss, water features, rocks, and twigs with crowns are just some of the ways to add nature features to your diorama. You can purchase moss, twigs, flowers, and vines at a dollar store. You can also gather items from a garden. Another idea is to use objects from a toy set or dollhouse. Use a small ball of clay to hold the objects upright, or glue them to the frame. An easy way to add nature elements is to cut pictures of trees, shrubs, and flowers from photos or magazines, and glue them to the back of the diorama to make the background.

MAKING AND ANCHORING TREES

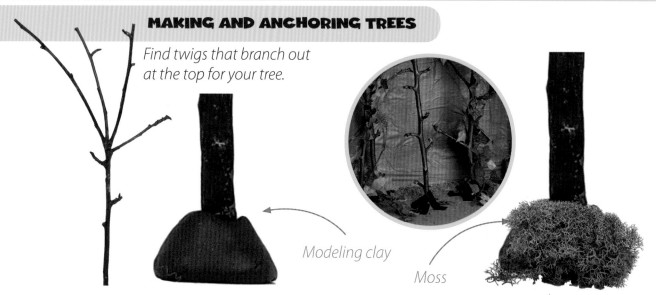

Find twigs that branch out at the top for your tree.

Modeling clay

Moss

For smaller trees, mold modeling clay into a cone shape. Press the twig into the clay. If it doesn't hold the twig straight, add more clay until it does.

When using taller trees in your diorama, glue or tape the bottom of the clay base to the base of your diorama so they don't fall over. You can then hide the base with rocks, pebbles, or moss.

To make decorative tree trunks, wrap your twigs in several layers of tissue paper and glue.

To make your tree more colorful, glue tiny pieces of tissue paper to your twigs to represent leaves or flowers.

TIP

Collect real pebbles to use as pathways and as a way to include nature elements in your diorama.

WORKING WITH MOSS

Use moss to create lifelike foliage for trees.

Tear the moss into sections.

Hang the moss on a twig or glue it in place.

ADDING VINES

Purchase vines at a dollar store, or collect small-leafed shoots from a garden.

Tape one end of the vine to the bottom of a tree trunk, and coil it around the trunk toward the top as shown. Use clear tape to hold the top of the vine in place.

CREATING WATER FEATURES

If you are planning to include water features in your diorama, you don't have to use actual water, which can be messy. There are several easy ways to create great-looking water effects that look almost real. Add small pebbles or pieces of grass around the edges for a more natural look.

*Fill a small, shallow container with colored sand. Using sand is great when you want your figures look partially **submerged** in water, just like the alligator above.*

Glue blue tissue or crepe paper to the base.

Cover the blue tissue paper strip with blue glass beads for a shiny, reflective look.

Another way to create a water feature is to paint the base of the diorama, or glue photos of water to the bottom.

Use thin, shredded paper strips to create the look of a fast-moving river.

CREATING BUILDINGS

Many dioramas include models of buildings or other structures. For example, if you are building a diorama of a city, you will need buildings and houses of various sizes. If you are reproducing a historical scene, you will want to create structures that look like the buildings of that time period. Buildings and structures are usually shaped like rectangles or cones. Here are instructions for creating them!

MAKING RECTANGULAR STRUCTURES

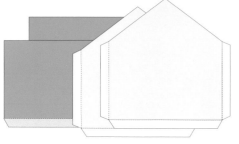  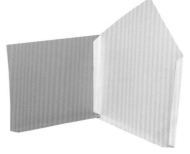

Use the pattern on page 30. Trace the pieces onto card stock, then cut them out. You will need one piece each for the front and the back of the house, and two pieces for the sides.

Draw and cut out windows and doors.

***Score** the paper along the dotted lines, then fold it. Glue or tape the tabs together. Start by attaching one side to the back of the house.*

Glue or tape the other side to the back of the house.

Glue or tape the front side to the two sides of the house.

Measure and cut a 10" x 6" (25.5 x 15 cm) rectangle out of cardboard. Fold it in half, and glue or tape it to the top of the house for the roof.

TIP

Scoring paper before folding it gives you a crisp, clean fold. You can use the tip of a dried-up pen or a very dull knife to score the paper.

Creative Huddle

You can create houses of any size by changing the dimensions of the house panels and roof.

MAKING CONICAL STRUCTURES

You can use these instructions for things such as teepees, castle **spires**, and roofs. The triangular shape can be used for Egyptian pyramids, too.

CONE SHAPE

Cut out a circle. Fold the circle in half, then in half again. Cut out one quarter section. Form a cone, and glue where the two cut edges overlap.

TIP

You can choose to decorate your structure in many different ways:

- *Paint the structure.*
- *Glue pieces of bark to the walls and straw to the roof to make the buildings look old.*
- *Glue pasta tiles to the roof.*
- *Glue scraps of cloth to the sides of a teepee to make it look more realistic.*

PYRAMID SHAPE

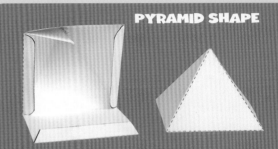

Use the pattern on page 31 to trace and cut out a square pyramid to use as a roof.

MAKE A TEEPEE

1 *Make a base for the teepee using the template on page 31. Use a hole punch to put 8 holes where indicated on the template.*

2 *Glue 8 skewer sticks or thin dowels to the holes. Tie them together at the top with string.*

3 *Cut a teepee shape from paper or cloth using the pattern on page 31. Decorate it. Wrap it around the poles and glue it together.*

HISTORICAL SCENES

A Native American group diorama is an artistic way of capturing the lifestyle of a specific group. Research information about a particular type of Native North American Nation, such as the Plains peoples or the Pueblo peoples. For example, when designing a scene in the Great Plains of North America, use an authentic setup of the plains. The Plains peoples lived in wide, open spaces, but they often camped in valleys with trees and a water source nearby.

Use the pyramid shape to create dioramas about ancient Egypt. Use breadcrumbs for great looking sand dunes.

NATURE SCENE
RAINFOREST DIORAMA

Tropical rainforests can be found near the **equator**. They are home to half the plant and animal species on Earth. The environment of tropical rainforests is lush, warm, and wet all year long. The average temperature in tropical rainforests ranges from 70 to 86 °F (21–30 °C). Tropical rainforests are so large that they are divided into four zones. Each zone forms an individual ecosystem where different animals and plants thrive. The emergent layer is the highest zone, followed by the canopy, then the understory, and finally the forest floor on the bottom. Try making your tropical rainforest diorama using tree branches and moss. It is an easy and fun-to-do project. Use these pages as inspiration, then add your own choice of materials!

See page 7 for the materials needed for this type of diorama.

1 You can build a simple set for your diorama using a cardboard box. Remove the lid, lay the box on its side, and cut the top part as shown above. Cut pieces of tissue paper and glue them to the inside of the box to create a colorful background.

2 Prepare several tree trunks as shown on page 18. First, place two taller trees at the back of the diorama platform, to form the emergent layer. Tear up pieces of dried moss and place them at the top of the tree trunks to form **tree crowns**.

3 Place several shorter tree trunks in front of the tall trunks, and anchor them to the platform. Wrap vines around the trunks as shown on page 19.

4 Tear up pieces of dried moss and place them on top of the shorter tree trunks to form tree crowns for the canopy layer of your rainforest.

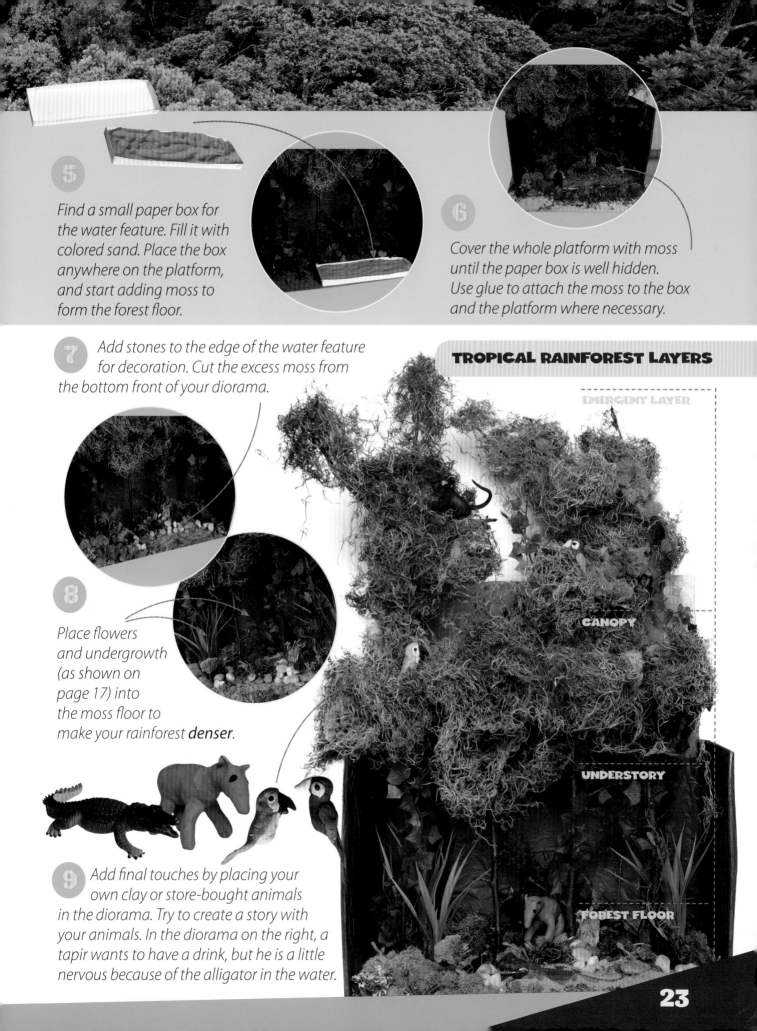

5 Find a small paper box for the water feature. Fill it with colored sand. Place the box anywhere on the platform, and start adding moss to form the forest floor.

6 Cover the whole platform with moss until the paper box is well hidden. Use glue to attach the moss to the box and the platform where necessary.

7 Add stones to the edge of the water feature for decoration. Cut the excess moss from the bottom front of your diorama.

8 Place flowers and undergrowth (as shown on page 17) into the moss floor to make your rainforest **denser**.

9 Add final touches by placing your own clay or store-bought animals in the diorama. Try to create a story with your animals. In the diorama on the right, a tapir wants to have a drink, but he is a little nervous because of the alligator in the water.

TROPICAL RAINFOREST LAYERS

EMERGENT LAYER

CANOPY

UNDERSTORY

FOREST FLOOR

LITERACY SCENE
ALICE IN WONDERLAND DIORAMA

Lewis Carroll wrote Alice in Wonderland in 1865. Since then, the story has been adapted for films, TV shows, cartoons, stage shows, comic books, and even an opera! The story follows the adventures of Alice who falls through a rabbit hole into a fantasy world. The fantasy world has many odd characters, including the White Rabbit, the Caterpillar, the March Hare, the Mad Hatter, and the Dormouse. The incredible setting and characters make this a great subject for a diorama.

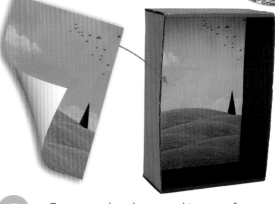

See page 7 for the materials needed for this type of diorama.

1 Build a simple set for your diorama using a cardboard box. Paint the outside and inside walls of the box.

2 Cut out a background image from a magazine, or print a photo using a color printer. Measure the inside of your box, and trim the image to match that size. Use glue or double-sided tape to stick it to the back of the box.

3 Prepare your paper characters (as shown on page 10). Use glue or double-sided tape to attach the tab of the cat to the top of the box. (See the cutouts on page 32.)

4 Use glue or double-sided tape to attach the fold along the tree to the side of the box.

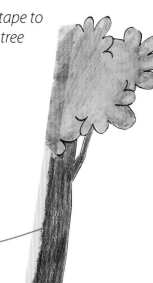

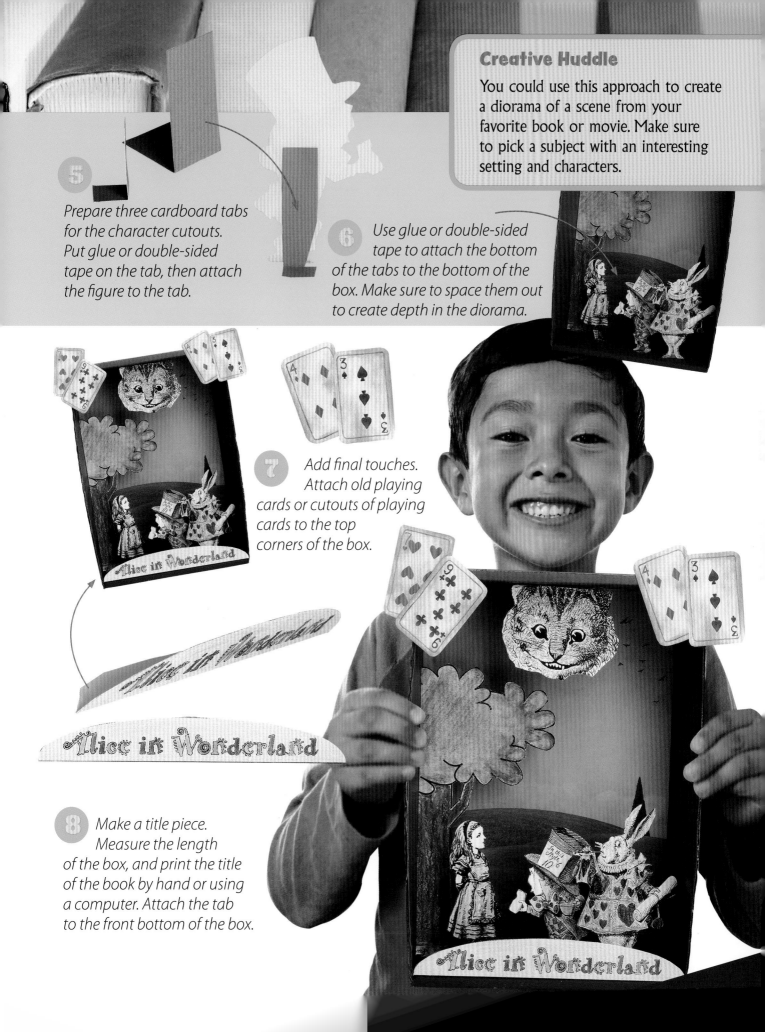

5 Prepare three cardboard tabs for the character cutouts. Put glue or double-sided tape on the tab, then attach the figure to the tab.

6 Use glue or double-sided tape to attach the bottom of the tabs to the bottom of the box. Make sure to space them out to create depth in the diorama.

7 Add final touches. Attach old playing cards or cutouts of playing cards to the top corners of the box.

8 Make a title piece. Measure the length of the box, and print the title of the book by hand or using a computer. Attach the tab to the front bottom of the box.

COMMUNITY SCENE

YOUR FAVORITE DOG PARK MODEL

A dog park is a park where dogs can run freely to get exercise without a leash. Many cities have dog parks that include treed areas, exercise equipment, benches for owners, and other features. The parks are usually surrounded by a fence to keep the dogs safe. There is also a gate to enter the park. Some parks even include a pond for the dogs to swim in and cool off! This project shows you how to create your favorite dog park.

See page 7 for the materials needed for this type of diorama.

1 *Start with the base platform for your diorama. Use the collage method to cover a piece of cardboard with green tissue paper.*

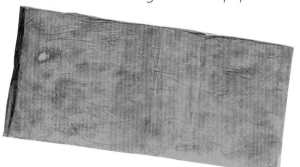

2 *Make an entrance to the park by cutting a half-circle shape out of cardboard. Cut a bone shape and glue that at the top. Cover with paper mache. When dry, paint the structure. If you decide to position your gate on the corner, angle the posts as shown below.*

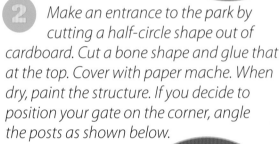

3 *Create and paint your paper mache hillside, hoop rings, climbing tower, and tunnel shapes (see page 13).*

4 *Make the umbrellas by cutting a paper mache ball in half. Paint each half a different color. Glue a small ball of modeling clay inside the ball, then stick a painted stir stick into the clay. Make another small ball of clay for the base.*

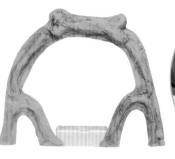

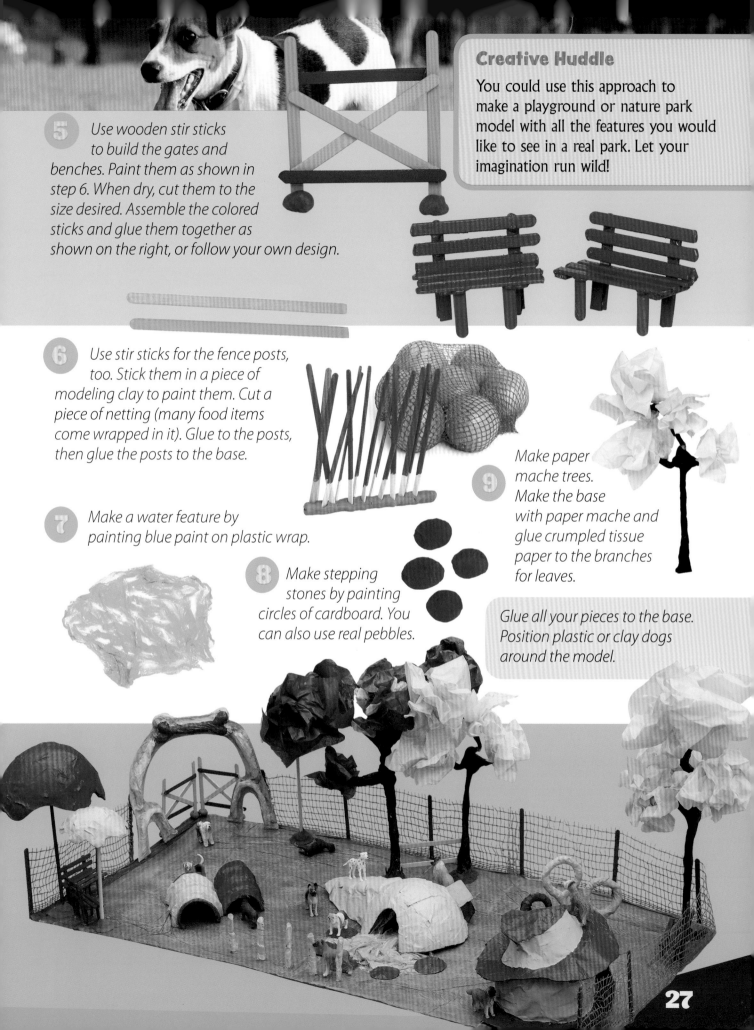

5 Use wooden stir sticks to build the gates and benches. Paint them as shown in step 6. When dry, cut them to the size desired. Assemble the colored sticks and glue them together as shown on the right, or follow your own design.

Creative Huddle

You could use this approach to make a playground or nature park model with all the features you would like to see in a real park. Let your imagination run wild!

6 Use stir sticks for the fence posts, too. Stick them in a piece of modeling clay to paint them. Cut a piece of netting (many food items come wrapped in it). Glue to the posts, then glue the posts to the base.

9 Make paper mache trees. Make the base with paper mache and glue crumpled tissue paper to the branches for leaves.

7 Make a water feature by painting blue paint on plastic wrap.

8 Make stepping stones by painting circles of cardboard. You can also use real pebbles.

Glue all your pieces to the base. Position plastic or clay dogs around the model.

CONSTRUCTION SCENE

YOUR DREAM HOUSE MODEL

Architects often create models of their buildings to show what they will look like. You can do the same thing! Start by thinking about what kind of house or building you would like to make. It doesn't have to be realistic—use your imagination! Then use the ideas on these pages to create your dream house or building.

See page 7 for the materials needed for this type of diorama.

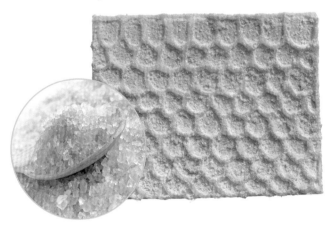

1 Cut out the house pieces using the pattern on page 30. Cut all the windows and doors you want the house to have.

2 Add "glass" to the windows by taping plastic wrap to the back of the window holes. For a stained glass effect, glue pieces of tissue paper to the inside wall window.

3 Paint the roof white. Add texture by covering it with glue, then sprinkling it with colored salt. (See page 7 for the instructions.) To add more texture, make ridges with the glue by squeezing it out in lines across the roof. When the roof is dry, glue it to the house.

4 Add a tower to the side of the house. Cut out the rectangle shape using the pattern on page 30. Add a pyramid roof as shown on page 21. Add shingles cut from a cardboard roll and glued to the pyramid. Cover the shingles with glue and sprinkle blue salt over them.

TIP Use coarse sandpaper for a different kind of texture for the roof. You could use a whole sheet of sandpaper folded in half, or cut out individual shingles and glue them to the roof to create a more realistic look.

Creative Huddle

You could use this approach to create a model of a place of worship, a castle, a farm, or an apartment building. You can also create a model of a historical building.

5 Make a porch with a roof that hangs over it. Use colored card stock or wrap colored construction paper around a piece of cardboard. The porch roof should be the same width as the front of the house. Make sure to leave enough paper to create a tab to attach the porch roof to the house.

6 Make supporting posts for the porch by making small paper rectangles like the tower. Cut the top into four tabs. Glue the tabs to the underside of the porch roof.

7 Use cardboard to make a base for the model. Paint a road at one end of the base. Use the collage method to cover the rest. Glue the house and tower to the base using the tabs on the bottom of the house. Glue the porch in front. Place the overhang on the porch and glue it to the house.

8 Use cardboard to make a picket fence. Cut out fence pickets. Cut out long narrow strips and glue the pickets to the strips. Glue the bottom of the pickets to the base.

9 Add final details and decorations. Glue pasta to the doors for door handles. Make a front path out of rice. Add bushes, trees, and store-bought or your own clay figurines.

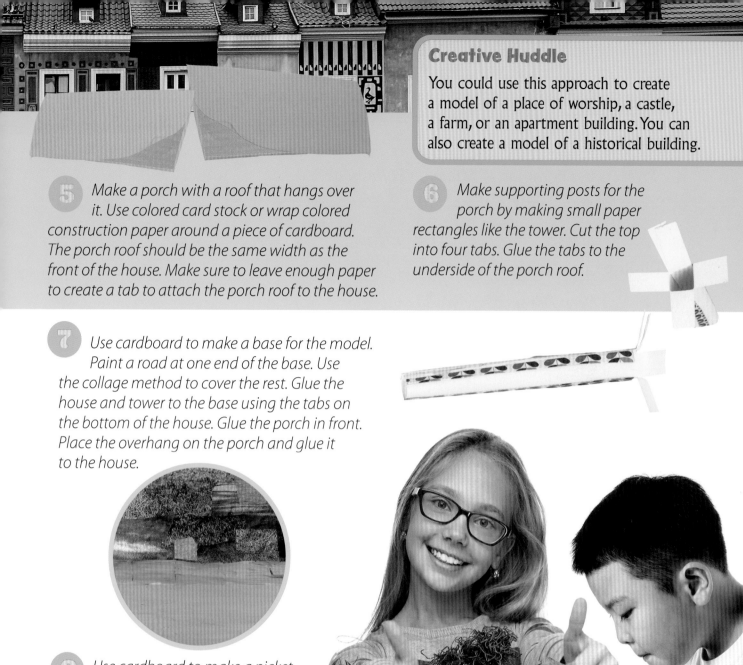

LEARNING MORE

Books

A+ Projects & Dioramas: A Student's Handbook
by SceneARama, SceneARama, 2010.

Build It: Invent New Structures and Contraptions
by Tammy Enz, Capstone Press, 2012.

If You Lived Here: Houses of the World
by Giles Laroche, HMH Books for Young Readers, 2011.

Websites

Storm the Castle
www.stormthecastle.com/shoebox_diorama/index_shoeboxdiorama.htm
Ideas for types of shoebox dioramas.

First Palette
www.firstpalette.com/Craft_themes/dioramas.html
Step-by-step instructions for creating a variety of dioramas.

WIKI HOW to do anything
www.wikihow.com/Make-a-Diorama
A step-by-step guide on how to make a diorama.

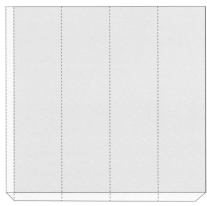

Tower, on page 28

Fold along the dotted lines, and tape or glue the tabs as needed.

Pattern for the house structure on pages 20 and 28

Note: These templates are reduced to 25 percent of the original size. Use a scanner or a printer to enlarge the templates to 400 percent.

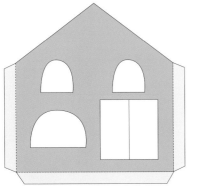

**House
Front piece**

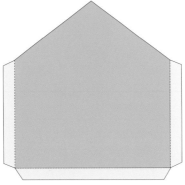

**House
Back piece**

**House
Side piece**

GLOSSARY

authentic Real and accurate

complex Complicated

dense Having objects that are close together, crowded

dilute Using water to make a liquid thinner

diorama A 3-D scene that fits inside a frame

ecosystem All of the things that live together in a particular environment

equator An imaginary line that goes around the middle of Earth, dividing it into two halves, called the northern hemisphere and the southern hemisphere

habitat A special place where a plant or animal lives

perpendicular At right angles to another object

representation Something that stands for something else

score To make a light indent in something such as paper

spire A tall tower often seen on castles

submerged Covered in water

tree crown The upper branches and leaves of a tree

three-dimensional (3-D) Something that has height, width, and depth

Pattern for the teepee on page 21

Canvas

Base

Pattern for the pyramid structure on page 21

Note: These templates are scaled to 50 percent of the original size. Use a scanner or a printer to enlarge the templates to 200 percent.

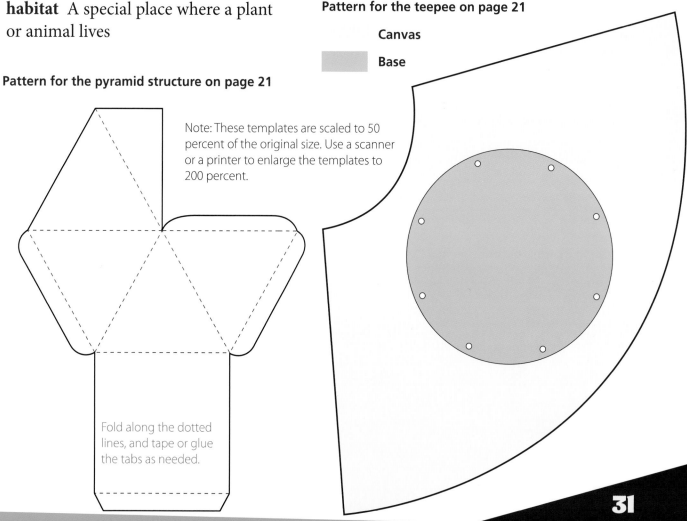

Fold along the dotted lines, and tape or glue the tabs as needed.

INDEX

Cutouts for the Alice in Wonderland diorama on page 24

Note: Use a scanner or a printer to resize the cutouts to the size you prefer, then color them.